HIS
Everlasting
WORD

HIS *Everlasting* WORD

Cherie E. Davis

XULON PRESS

Xulon Press
2301 Lucien Way #415
Maitland, FL 32751
407.339.4217
www.xulonpress.com

© 2019 by Cherie E. Davis

All rights reserved solely by the author. The author guarantees all contents are original and do not infringe upon the legal rights of any other person or work. No part of this book may be reproduced in any form without the permission of the author. The views expressed in this book are not necessarily those of the publisher.

Unless otherwise indicated, Scripture quotations taken from the King James Version (KJV)–*public domain.*

Printed in the United States of America.

ISBN-13: 978-1-5456-7668-4

Dedication

I thank my Lord and Savior for the inspiration of this book, as well as family and friends.

Contents

Introduction ix

1. Your Grace Is Sufficient...................................1
2. Because of You..3
3. I Can Always Count on You 4
4. Confidence..5
5. Don't You Know?..7
6. For All of My Sisters around the World...................9
7. For You, Father... 16
8. For You, Mother... 18
9. Forgiveness... 19
10. Give Me... 20
11. He Made You.. 21
12. Heaven Only Knows...................................... 22
13. I'm Still Here.. 24
14. I Forgot to Pray 26
15. I Have Always Been There............................... 28
16. I Love You Because..................................... 30
17. I Will Trust You 31
18. Is This Really True Love?.............................. 32
19. Judgement Will Come 34
20. Know His Strength 36
21. Let Me Hide Away....................................... 37
22. Life... 38
23. Look Up and Live....................................... 39

24.	Love Has Been So Nice	40
25.	My Soul Reaches Out	41
26.	One Dark Day (Short Story)	43
27.	Resurrection	58
28.	Silent Tears	60
29.	Sistas	61
30.	So Long Ago	63
31.	Standing by the Ocean Side	64
32.	The Evidence of Love	66
33.	The Light of Love	67
34.	The Longer You Hold My Heart	68
35.	To All of My Brothers and Sisters	69
36.	Turn Around, Turn Around	70
37.	Understanding	71
38.	Waiting	73
39.	Where Are You, My Brothers?	74
40.	Where Did Our Love Go?	75
41.	With Open Arms	76
42.	Without You	77
43.	Worthy of Love	78

Quotes for the Day 80
Epilogue: Let's Be Real 83

Introduction

I see so many lives and families being torn apart, for one reason or another. So many people lost in this devastating world with no faith, no hope, and no love, looking for love in all the wrong places. Maybe one day in your life, you had found the Lord, then something or someone came your way and you felt that the joy you once knew was gone—unspeakable pain. You left your first love, Jesus, to whom you had given your life.

You may feel Christ is no longer needed in your life. Well, Jesus says, "Without Me, there is no hope; without Me, you can do nothing." For me, that speaks volumes. So come back to your first love, the Lord, where you can find love, peace, and joy. It's not difficult; He makes it plain. Will you surrender all? Christ is waiting for you! We will all see the King of Glory real soon. Are you ready to meet the Bridegroom?

May these words of the Holy Spirit inspire you, and may He be the keeper of your house. Along with the inspirational poetry that I realize was guided by the Holy Spirit, I also wanted to share some love poems, letting you know what real love could possibly be when you fall in love. Yet you must fall in love with your Heavenly Father first.

Everyone needs someone to love. After all, the Lord made someone in this life for you to love. If you haven't found that special someone to love, start with loving yourself first. Christ will show you how to love by acknowledging Him and reading His holy Scriptures. Then you will know real love and be convinced that you can share this love with another—with the one He made just for you. May Christ be the open mystery of your life.

Your Grace Is Sufficient

I walk in this life that You, Lord, have given me...
Trials and tribulations have I endured. At times, I didn't know
where my life would go. Your grace is sufficient.
As I live this life, gathering things made of men's hands...
This I understand. Yet! I still am empty inside. This is why.
I gathered the possessions in a make-believe world...
Filling my soul in sheer delight, not realizing all
I needed was You... You are mine, and Your grace is sufficient.
I grazed on the self-gratification of my wealth and material
gain, hearing the rhythm and the intense beating of my heart...
I couldn't find You there.

I picked up the Bible and read a scripture...
For what shall a man profit, if he shall gain the whole world, and
lose his own soul? Or what shall a man exchange for his soul?
We don't know where the wind cometh and where it may blow...
One thing that is for sure: Christ has full control...
As time unfolds, I gave the tainted life I knew and said...
Your grace is sufficient. Everywhere I go, I speak the truth
that only is mastered and given by You...
No matter, when all hell breaks loose, all knowledge and wisdom
inspired by You, You promised us Your love and Your grace would
be sufficient.

Christ will be there for you when that darkest hour descends upon the earth. Will you remember the one verse that said, "When I come back, will I find faith"?

I will give you the power in the finale hour...

For those who carried their cross and walked with Me, never to give up, as the day draws near, I, Christ, am the only one to fear...

For you, My grace is sufficient.

Because of You

Because I found You in the beginning of my life,
I never knew love could be so wonderful. You are the inspiration of
every day I love. Because of You, life is more meaningful.
This is why I love. Oh! Because of You, I can smile.
Every day, I learn how to trust You, believe in You, have faith…
No matter what comes my way, I'm living for today,
because of You.

Life without You is such a lonely road; down it, I never want to go.
Because of You, brighter and righter is each day with You.
You are the air I breathe, You are my everything, You are the reason
why I sing… You are my constant dream.

Because of You, You will be all I need... How could I have found a
love so true?
I'll do anything for You… You are mine. In my soul You are. I am
forever in love with You, and it's all because of You.

I Can Always Count on You

I can always count on You when the darkest
moment meets up with time...
This is the Son, and His light will shine... His presence
is finally seen to all that have believed,
even to the ones that never believed.
Don't wait until you see the sky fade away,
seeing the splendor of our majesty, our King,
returning to the earth to receive His bride to be...
This will be the most beautiful event in all of history.
Christ's story was told a thousand times over....
Pick up your Bibles and erase your doubt...
You don't want to be lost
and turned out into utter darkness,
where there is no escape.
Don't you want to stand at heaven's gate,
sitting at marriage supper of the Bridegroom,
where He made room for all those that were chosen?
Do you want to take that chance on something
you are not sure of?
a soul damned for all eternity wasn't God's plan
for any man...
Christ is coming to gather His holy people,
without spot or blemish or winkle.
Are you ready to hear His cry in the midnight hour?
So to pretend there will be no end,
I believe I can count on Him.

Confidence

The confidence is what I strive daily to walk...
As we know, life isn't easy.
The road that we travel may sometimes may be rough...
Can we see or know what's at the end?
My confidence is to realize that
Christ will always be there by my side...
Don't dwell on things you don't understand...
Be grateful and willing to live by His commandments
of which you must take hold!
Our Master in heaven knows the beginning and the plans for every man.
The confidence is to know that He alone has in His heart
for every man His designed plan.
Spread over time for me and you, He lives His life in His truth.
He said He would come back and receive His own...
Zion! Keep His laws bedded deep down in your souls.
He is the only one that has been given full control,
so stand righteously for His Word alone.
Faith in that day is what we should keep,
No matter what's going on around you.
When you hear the voice of our Savior's call,
will you be lost and know nothing at all?
The confidence, my love, when you hear the trumpet blow
and watch the sky roll up in a scroll...
Have the confidence to trust... He will do the rest.
Get your souls prepared because this is a test.

Ask yourself... Do you know when time is no more?
Our Father is coming back to even the score.
The confidence is to know within your heart
What part in life you played...
Do you have the living water today?
It's the confidence to say, "Lord, I'm ready
for You to take my life today."

Don't You Know?

Don't you know when I divided the heavens,
I made someone to bring it together?
We threw the sun, moon, and stars to
show we are infinite as one...
Don't you know destiny is at its peak?
I'm not here to make you weak,
For every man will bow his knee.
Don't you know I thought of you before time began?
You can't even number the grains of sand.
As days go by, they stayed the same.
I only changed the color in a frame.
Soon everyone will call out My name.
Come to me, you who are humble and weak,
Dedicate your souls—that's required of thee.
I will show you the things that will be,
for I am heavenly.
Don't you know I'm coming soon?
Open up your hearts and make room.
Yes! I'm Jesus, the Bridegroom,
bringing My saints to the upper room,
where I have prepared a place real soon.
Don't worry about today, for it's sufficient, enough;
Gather your Bibles that are cracked with dust.
Haven't you known I love you this much?
Don't you know it's I you should trust?

His Everlasting Word

I made every bird and creeping thing...
Won't you see this love I bring?
To set the record straight,
Yes, I have many golden gates.
Don't you know My arms are open wide
for every man, woman, and tribe?
I give life bought with a price, not a bribe.
My everlasting glory is for me as I adored thee.
I'm neither where you can come and see;
in the secret chambers, I will never be.
Don't you know My place is holier
than you have ever known it to be...
I have the keys everlasting.
I'm in your hearts so secretly...
Place your sights on things above.
My sweet child, I'm blissful and love.
I have the hour and the power as I sit here,
awaiting in My majestic tower.
Don't you know when I get my command
how many men will be able to stand?

FOR ALL OF MY SISTERS AROUND THE WORLD

So! Let me begin…
Many of us see ourselves wanting to be that perfect mate,
hoping that we have enough love in our hearts to share
with another,
that the Most High will present to us men
if we will just wait on Him.
If we want to be chosen by a man after our Savior's heart,
a man who is willing to live in all of His ways,
then that is the man you want coming for your heart and time.
These days, I know that sounds like a complete fairytale.
There are many women who don't know
to whom they should give their heart and love;
many feel it's just a waste of time.
For me, I have always wanted to be someone who knew how to
love the right way.
The only way that is accomplished is by living in the righteous
acts of our Creator.

"Whoever pursues righteousness and love finds life, prosperity and honor." – Proverbs 21:21

"But seek first his kingdom and his righteousness, and all these things will be given to you as well." – Matthew 6:33

"The eyes of the Lord are on the righteous, and his ears are attentive to their cry." – Psalm 34:15

"Finally, brothers and sisters, whatever is true, whatever is noble, whatever is right, whatever is lovely, whatever is admirable—if anything is excellent or praiseworthy, think about such things." – Philippians 4:8

Honestly, that is the way I want to present myself to our heavenly Father. I have always adored the thought falling in love, but then I had to first fall in love with Christ in order to love someone else. So, ladies, it's not always that we have chosen the wrong man; oftentimes, we have to let our light shine so the Most High can draw the right man.

"Love must be sincere. Hate what is evil, cling to what is good. Be devoted to one another in love. Honor one another above yourselves." – Romans 12:9-10

"A friend loves at all times." – Proverbs 17:17

"Love is patient, love is kind. It does not envy, it does not boast, it is not proud. It does not dishonor others, it is not self-seeking, it is not angered, it keeps no record of wrongs. Love does not delight in evil but rejoices with the truth. It always protects, always trusts, always hopes, always perseveres. Love never fails." – Corinthians 13:4-8

"'The most important one,' answered Jesus, 'Is this: hear, o Israel: the Lord, the Lord is one. Love the Lord your God with all your heart and with all your soul and with all your mind and with

all yourself. There is no commandment greater than these.'" –
Mark 12: 29-31

You can have a Godly relationship with the opposite sex through friendship, but you have to keep it clean and real with the Most High, in order for Him to be a part of the union of matrimony, if that is your choice. Always be praying and hoping for the best, which will only come from our heavenly Father.

If we don't put the Lord first, in times like these, we will need a Savior because the outcome can end in being lost and in despair. Often, we will not realize that if we had waited on the Most High, we could gain the truest of a man's heart from our Savior. With this man, in no doubt will you love to spend all eternity, because you waited on the gift of love from our Creator.

Christ gave me a heart to love, and that in itself can be rewarding. Sometimes we feel we didn't end up with the love of our life, and we may wonder if we waited on the Lord to provide that man. At times, no! We moved ahead of our Father and settled for what we thought was best for us, not knowing it could be a mistake on our part. You can lose yourself along the way, believing and trusting someone who says they love you, then finding out that you are left with a broken heart. Always trust the Word of our Lord and Savior, for He will never lie to you.

"Trust in the Lord with all your heart, and do not lean on your own understanding."

"Delight yourself in the Lord, and He will give you the desires of your heart. Commit your way to the Lord; trust in him, and he will act. He will bring forth your righteousness as a light, and your justice as the noonday." – Psalm 37: 4-6

Romans 8:28

"You keep him in perfect peace whose mind is stayed on you, because he trusts in you." – Psalm 37: 5

"And without faith it is impossible to please him, for whoever draw near to God must believe he exists and that he rewards those who seek him."

"Fear not, for I am with you; be not dismayed, for I am your God; I will strengthen you, I will help you, I will uphold you with my righteous right hand." – Isaiah 41:10

Psalm 91:1-16

Sometimes, we as women live our lives through other people, when we should be a pillar of faith for all women. We should be walking after God's heart.

Never be afraid to reach out for that higher calling, that is instrumental in our faith walk with the Most High God. When you feel the enemy is tempting you, remember:

"No temptation has overtaken you except what is common to mankind. And God is faithful; He will not let you be tempted *beyond what you can bear. But when you are tempted, He will also provide a way out so that you can endure it." – 1 Corinthians 10: 13*

It's true when Christ said: "It is not good for man too be alone." Well, there are some people who will move ahead of God, when God wants the work to be done in our lives for Him. Remember sisters, God has called a lot of us so our election will be made sure in Him. If we are called, our lives will be anointed by Him. So, remember, we are not alone when Christ has caused you to be about His mission and work; He has called you and will be with you. Don't feel like you can't find love; let love find you.

"A man that finds a wife finds a good thing and obtains favor from the Lord." – Proverbs 18:22

Never fail to remember that Christ said, "I will never leave you nor forsake you."

As long as you have breath in your bodies, know that our Savoir has our back, so we don't have to look back and wonder if we are loved by anyone on this earth.

Let yourself be validated only by what the Lord feels about your walk for Him. Do not look for any validation in what mankind thinks about you. Make sure you understand that the only thing that matters is who has full control of your life. If it's a husband that you seek, let him be the choice of the Most High. The only way to be sure about your husband is to ask yourself, "What is his walk with the Most High? Is he is a representation of the Most High? Would he be all pleasing to God?"

Don't give up on what the Most High first founded marriage upon in the Garden of Eden. All things He made are very good. So wait on the Lord!

Let your soul run after Christ and pick up that cross and finish your race for Him. Let Him renew your faith in Him. So wait on the Lord, and make sure that man who is coming for your heart is grounded in Christ.

"But they who wait for the Lord shall renew their strength, they shall mount up with wings like eagles; they shall run and not faint." – Isaiah 40:31

"Rest in the Lord and wait patiently for Him, do not fret because of Him who prospers in His way because of the man who carries out wicked schemes." – Psalm 37:7

"Behold, as the eyes of our Lord look to the Lord our God, until He is gracious to us." – Psalm 123:2

"Therefore the Lord longs to be gracious to you. And therefor he waits on high to have compassion on you. For the Lord is a God of justice." – Isaiah 30:18

"And not only this, but also we ourselves, having the first fruits of the spirit, even we ourselves groan within ourselves, waiting eagerly for our adoption as sons, the redemption of our body. For in hope we have been saved, but if we hope for what he already sees? But if we hope for what we already see, with perseverance we wait eagerly for it." – Romans 8:23-25

Keep steadfast in your walk for the Most High, for He alone is able to keep you in all of His ways. His extension of His mighty hand can be with you forever, if you are willing to trust and have faith. Believe He will never let you go. How blessed are those who long for Him.

As long as you are willing to hold His precious hand, may Christ always be the keeper of your house, for all eternity.

FOR YOU, FATHER

For surely there is peace in every move he makes,
as he takes the road to a higher plain.
I am asking You, Father, to show him the way,
guiding his footsteps along the way.
In his mouth only, wisdom speaks of You!
The things that he knows were foretold many years ago.
His mind, his heart, his soul, only You know!
Let others be captivated by his spirit,
for it is of years of daily seeking, seeking You,
spreading the Good News everywhere he goes...
And yet, he knows! He continues to give You, Christ,
full control of his life... A Love so true! Father, You knew.
This soul goes and goes, and You know!
Down that rocky road, it may be hard to climb and bare,
but with Thine love, he will find more understanding in all his days!
You, Father, took his hand one day and said,
"Come, walk and talk all about Me,
For I am the power—a love that overpowers
in any space and time!"
The universe unknown to men, the universal mysteries only
he speaks of
as life carries him on, and he is set forth...
For Your love, Father, is forever in his spirit...
All those that can, will hear it, fear it.
You, Father, sit upon the center of the earth;

this is something You put inside of me at birth.
I've found Your way; within my Heart, You stay,
beside me everywhere I travel and go each day.
You are with me, for Your love, Father, is more than a mystery.
This is why I will always believe...

For You, Mother

The Light of Love came and touched your heart...
You'll soon see the Creation of love that was meant to be.
Into this life you were born...
I will love and love you forevermore.
So the life that was given to you,
you learned how to love continuously,
cherishing, remembering a mother's love
straight from heaven,
this is the sweetness of a mother's love.
Most of all, in everything, the Most High gave us you.
The Light of Love came and touched our hearts.
On this day we share the life, the love
that was given from above.
I can't say that I won't cry!
On this day, we celebrate the life we knew...
For you, mother! We will never say goodbye,
for you were wise. Now, your spirit ascends to the heavens,
where you await the resurrection.
We are guarded by His power!
The grace of God will never take you where the grace of God
cannot keep you.
This is for you, mother, the Light of our Love.

Forgiveness

Far above the heavens that I cannot see,
oceans spread wide and deepen in the crystal blue sea.
This is the kind of depth of love that the Lord has for us,
and only He will know.
Within His power, all things were created...
He sits upon the circle of the earth
and gathers all of Israel with faith and trust.
I stand before You, Lord... Humble and true.
We don't realize why we're loved so much by You.
Because it wasn't human hands that made us.
The infinite One that took flight long ago, as we fight for our lives.
It's not human hands that paved the way. It's Christ who showed
us His way.
When you go knocking on the door to His heart,
Make sure that forgiveness is steadfast in your heart.
He came into your heart, and you believe it's just a dream
that the world calls make believe.
The darkest hour in all of its power will soon descend on
the earth.
So I say, did you pray?
Did you forgive any man today?
This is the exceptional time of year
to get it right before He draws near.
Love, faith, trust, and forgiveness, it's clear!

GIVE ME

Give me your eyes, so I can see what's deep inside.
Give me your mind, so I can once again find
the inner mystery, locked away and true.
Give me your smile, so I can sit and stare awhile.
Give your touch... I'm giving you this much.

Give me your pain; I'll show you can love again.
Give me your arms wrapped around my soul.
I want to lose control
in your love, your eyes
In all and everything that's new,
just give me you.

He Made You

You are guarded by His power, the grace of Yah!
He will never take you where the grace of Yah cannot keep you...
So, as our strength comes from the joy of the Lord,
my sister, my sister, you are truly one He adores...
He made you...
to explore your destiny in life; now He has called you home...
Only you alone! He has set aside for His precious own
He made you...
Of course, there will be sadness, but there's a truth of gladness.
As you closed your eyes and saw His face with all of His glory
and grace,
you now stand in God's heavenly bliss.
He made you...
As I seal your face with a special kiss...
My sister, my sister! You won't be tired anymore;
it's Yah's kingdom you can now explore.

Heaven Only Knows

Heaven only knows what's in my heart.
I want to sing a song within my heart only Jesus knows…
A song of dreams coming true for me and you.
Close your eyes, meditate on His love…
You may hear the thunder of His voice so deep inside of you.
Look up! It's really true:
Christ died for me and you.
Heaven only knows, as He kisses the wind and brings angels from afar…
Heaven only knows what's in my heart.
He blows the trumpet, unlocks the winds…
It's not hard to understand, what's coming next;
we live in a time that's perplexed.
Lift up your minds, your heart.
Christ is the one who really knows the things about to unfold.
He holds the sun, moon, and stars…
Are you still doubting that He's the One who holds the future of a man?
Nothing comes covered; you won't understand.
Come! Walk, hold His extending hand, believe!
God does have a plan.

Heaven only knows you saw my work in visions and dreams…
You ask yourself, "Whose sweet voice could this be?"
I'm the man, Christ, who died on Calvary.

Heaven only knows…
I woke up in the early morning Son and said to myself, You are the One.

I'm giving my life to you.
Heaven only knows…
I don't want to awaken one day to see
all of life's realities
I threw away without a care
and question myself, "Are You still there
to see my life flash before my face?"
Now, I know I must run this race
to live life without His grace.
You and I will stand face to face…
Heaven only knows.

I'm Still Here

I waited for You, Lord, to show me Your love
that another could give.
You knew way before my time.
And now, I live with the disappointments, time after time.
I look to You once again.
I hear You say, "I'm still here."
Lord, it sometimes doesn't feel like I have a purpose.
I thought many times I would have to share...
My purpose at the surface isn't what I wanted it to be.
I look to the sky and ask You, "Why?"
I hear Your voice, and I begin to cry...
"I'm still here."
Many years have passed me by; I no longer can ask and wonder...
All this time, You had me for Yourself...
The wedding bells...
Gone down in history, the love of a wife joined hand in hand
with the trueness of one love, only one can understand.
We live and give all that we have...
Now it's just raindrops, puddled in the sand.
I look and ask You one more time,
who will be the man that will love me for a lifetime?
I hear Your voice, Lord, as You say to me...
"I am your husbandman! You are My bride.
I wipe away all tears from your eyes.
Come, sit at the marriage supper of the Lamb,

who shed His precious blood for all of man.
Let Me hold your hand… I do understand
your heart that is so complete in you…
You are My living proof that I, Christ, made room for you.
When you ask the question about My forever love…
I say to you now, 'I am still here.'"

I Forgot to Pray

The mystery of life that intensifies our daily lives...
Encountering the steps along the way, sometimes I...
Stood up; sometimes I fell!
One reality came rushing in:
I forgot to pray.
At times we don't realize what's ahead of us,
hoping we have the answers,
knowing in my spirit there's a higher calling...
I come to know.
Seeking Him often, there was something deep inside.
I could not get all emotional, the profound feeling...
This you will find: the Most High is capable of knowing our
deepest thoughts...
Why should we fear it? What's bought to our mind?
I forgot to pray.
Acknowledging your destiny in this life can be beautiful.
Put down your defenses and be persistent...
Accepting who you are... Amazing, isn't it?
Then come back and say...
"I forgot to pray."
A gift of love has been put in my heart...
He has been waiting on me to believe in myself...
That's my Savior who went
to bring all creation that belongs to Him,
that we have so long waited for His blessed appearance...

Christ will show up, show out,
some not knowing what's it's all about...
I forgot to pray.
Never forget that it was our Christ who went away
to prepare a place for us,
for His people, created in His image.
Now, His love diminished in the earth...
Your mission is to fight against the wales of the evil one.
It wasn't Christ who doubted my walk;
it is for me to pick up my cross
and say...
"I forgot to pray."

I Have Always Been There

My little one, can you remember when you were a child?
I walked with you for quite a while.
When your tears would fall, I caught them all...
Placed them inside My eyes, so I could quiet you, along the way.
I, Yah! I have made you to be strong.
You belong in My kingdom to come...
I am the One!
I have always been there...
As you stare at My surrounding beauty,
the fulfilment of the rainbow that's round about the atmosphere...
Here am I, the Most High!
Demands from all those that will see
the worship and praise that wisdom brings...
I have always been there.
I knew you before you came to be!
Keep walking and talking about My love,
the inner mysteries of Me...
I control the footsteps of every man that walks this earth.
The destiny that will surely be...
I told you, I am heavenly.
I, Yah, give to every man, woman, and child, a voice to
shout out loud.
Stand to the east and watch, I say, watch!
The story that was told so long ago...
It's about too unfold...

Hold on to all that's truth...
I have always been there.
I have come to you in visions and dreams...
Will you wake up and find out what I mean?
Then you will receive the kingdom that will come.
My Sabbath law commandments and statues are to abide by...
Won't you hear My cry?
I'm telling you,
I have always been there.
Never forget, I have forever loved you...
From the beginning of time,
you are the apple of My eye.
I hear your constant cry...
There's a reason why...
You'll forever be mine.
Look forward to your golden gate...
I, Yah, have longed for and await... Never stop loving Me as you do.
I have proven My love too all of you...
Remember...
I have always been there.

I Love You Because

I love because you made me cry
and knew someone that's wiser than I.
I love you because you made me see the completeness
of what love should really be...
To wake up and find you gone.
There is an inner being that made me strong.
My love for you wasn't wrong.
It just put me in a place where I truly belong...
Where I felt His touch.
Surely my Christ is full of splendor and magnificent
I love You because You formed me in my mother's womb,
just like You blew life into Larzarus, when You entered the tomb.
I love You because You have a people, ever grateful,
as we lift up holy hands to show we're faithful.
I love You because You gave us You,
to establish Your Kingdom, through and through.

I Will Trust You

The time is near.
What should I fear?
Where there's turmoil everywhere...
I will trust You...
I can run and hide and try to escape the day...
For all awaits Your coming,
knowing You will find me.
I will trust You...
Will You find me, fasting in prayer, being kind
too all those that are blind,
and refuse to open up their eyes and mind?
Finally, see and believe,
singing songs of Zion, never realizing,
we are the people, longing for that day,
as You went away too prepare a place,
I say I will trust You.

Is This Really True Love?

I saw you for the first time, and my heart skipped a beat.
Could this be sweet love for me?
Gather your thoughts; now listen.
I found solace in your touch, peace beneath my feet.
Is this love meant for me?
Everywhere I've walked, I've wondered,
Is this really true love?
Somewhere up above,
there's got to be this thing called love,
but how could this be
when you're gone away from me?
Destiny so incomplete,
Because in my heart I felt you were so right for me.
Now tears fall as rivers run deep.
I find myself asking questions:
"Is this really true love?"
Lost within my heart, I gave my heart to you…
What am I to do?
Trust and believe
You're still the one for me?
That's easy to do, if only you knew…
When I look in your eyes,
I see the disappointing times.
You ask yourself, "Why?"
Is it under the bridge of love?

You want to know,
Is this really true love?
I found joy and pain while standing out in the rain.
Thunder bolts, striking my heart,
tearing the profound love I once knew
All you do is sing the blues about me and you.
Is this really true love?
What is it?
You could have been in a dream state of mind.
Well, this is what I find:
Don't hold on to a heart that is no longer yours too keep,
because even under the sheets, you lied to me.
Love was supposed to be sweet;
how could this be?
I feel so deceived… Is this just a dream?
Remember, if you are yearning for a love that has no flaws,
it's not love you need at all.
It's like blowing a kiss in the invisible wind,
where in it, we know it has no end.
So be it! A fleeting moment of this love you feel, however
long it lasts.
Stop breaking me;
there's nothing more to seek.
Stop taunting and testing me…
set this love free.

Judgement Will Come

Israel, you have heard of My descent again, again, and again.
Set up the battleships, for the arrows will fly by day!
I, Yah, have shown you the time of the open door...
What do you think you have been living for?
Now comes the time for My glory to shine...
From one end of heaven, to the next of forever
The Most High Yah, our power, have the hour.
I will give My command where all in heaven stand
to bring all angels from afar.
Judgment will come.
Get ready for your deliverance to come...
Back to the beginning where it all started from.
Israel, I have given the land to you.
Here is the moment in time...
This is why you have been awakened to the truth...
The holy Bible that was given to only you.
Stop fighting over who's wrong or right.
Keep the laws, that is all.
I will seal My saints for all eternity...
I will not cast My holy Word in the bottom of the sea.
In My presence, you will finally see
My holy Word that was given for all eternity...
Stand strong, stand strong!
Judgement will come.
My salvation is given to those that are called.

When I come back, will I find faith, solely dedicated to Me?
I laid down My life on Calvary.
Seek wisdom and knowledge and understand
I am not coming back as man
I am coming back with all power in My hands…
The kingdom is only given to a few;
If you are living your life without Me, what will you do?
That will be the life you blew…
I've given you the gift of love!

That was thought out in the heavens above.
My sweet child, I am blissful and full of love.
Why do you keep longing for a world that will die?
Will you wait until you see the chariots in the sky?
Stand faithful, just, and true!
You must believe I am coming for you.
Israel, gather your hearts and place them together…
My praise, glory, and honor!
The world will see and believe.
Hold fast! I am coming real soon…
I told you, I am Christ, the Bridegroom!
Israel, the earth will I set afire.
This is My heart's desire.
I am that I am… The only King of Israel.

Know His Strength

Psalm 68:31-35

Princes shall come out of Egypt;
Ethiopia shall soon stretch out her hands unto god.
Sing unto God, you kingdoms of the earth;
o sing praises unto the Lord.
To him that rideth upon the heavens of heaven...
Rideth upon the which were of old.
Lo, he doth send out his voice, and that a mighty voice.
Acribe ye strength unto God;
his excellency is over Israel, and his strength is in the clouds.....
O God, thou art terrible out of thy holy places;
the God of Israel is he that giveth strength and power unto
his people.
Be blessed of God.

Let Me Hide Away

Let me hide away in Your heart, close to mine.
You've got the kind of love, oh Jesus, keeper of my soul.
This I know:
I can't live without You.
I don't want to be lost in a world...
With no hope, no joy, no love!
You are sent from above,
the Greatest love of all...
Let me hide away, where You can find me,
praying, fasting for You.
There's a place we like to go, reaching for our high calling...
Christ, our all and all.
Time will tell if we knew You...
I can't live without You.
There's a place we like to go... Heaven,
where He went away to prepare a place for you and me...
Please believe.
Let me hide away in Your heart, close to mine.
It won't be long now until we hear His shout from heaven:
"It is Done!"
Let me hide away in Your arms, where it's safe and warm.
I want to hide away in Your love.

LIFE

Life teaches us that we must go through the ups and downs
that make men and women out of me and you.
Life can throw us some powerful blows,
often, at times when have no control.
I'm only saying that God truly loves,
so put your trust and faith in the things above.
These are the things that Christ truly loves.
The truth isn't hard to see…
Christ did die for you and me,
to set the hearts of all men free.

Look Up and Live

Christ is fast approaching…
In my mind, I can no longer hide.
I took too long to run this race.
Today I say, I will look up and live.
I gathered as much as I could, not that I truly should,
realizing all I need is You, my Savior…
This world will never be enough
until I look up and live!
All the comforts of this life wouldn't promise me.
Only as I live for You…
What's promised when I go up in a beam of light…
I will look up and live.
It will be just a fleeting moment…
My life doesn't belong to me.
It is to give to my Brothers and Sisters
glimpse of what could be sweet love…
If you would…
Look up and live.

Love Has Been So Nice

Sure, we had our ups and downs...
We vowed to stay in love.
So let me say, love has been so nice.
Into the storm, you kept me warm...
Love has been so nice.
What we share is a special love,
where in the heavens, we know it is blessed upon.
Only a few will receive the truest of love meant to be...
Love has been so nice.
Sure, we've had our share of love's ups and downs...
In love, we have found you can make it,
if you reach for the Higher Caller that extends
love, life, without measure,
then you can be sure you will stay together.
Love has been so nice...
The greatest love of all.

My Soul Reaches Out

My soul reaches out too someone I've never seen…
And yet, I believe in a power the universe has never known.
Exploring the possible that seems impossible to mankind.
We needn't wonder any longer…
His power is displayed throughout the hemisphere.
Our sleeping soul awakes out of the dust where He has created us…
Who can I be speaking of?
The King of Glory, soon to return.
While the earth awakens to the voice of wisdom of everything.
It sways and blows upheavals all over the world…
No one knows when their soul will fly away.
Constantly reminding me, as my soul reaches out to claim
the life that our Lord has given us, as astounding as it is.
This will be all that we've waited for:
Exploring the possible that is now possible to man…
My soul reaches out; I will no longer be in any doubt..
My soul reaches out to the One who gave me life.
There is life in everything that breathes,
so when He breathed life into you and me,
it was no mistake.
Grab hold of His heavenly ways.
The days are shorter; the night is laid in darkness.
One day, it will be too late to say, "I now trust and believe."
Faith will be the only thing that can ride out the storm on the way.

Can you be sure Christ will be coming for you?
Give your life to Him today and say,
"My soul reaches out, because I found out what true love is all about...
Therefore, I will never live in doubt...
My soul reaches out."

One Dark Day (Short Story)

What's going on? I woke up to what seemed to be the end of time.

It's supposed to be morning; instead, it's the afternoon... *How could this happen?*

Did I sleep the morning away? Apparently so... *That's not what I usually do.*

I rushed to unplug my phone. There was nothing, it was charged, but no connection.

I turned the television on; it was slightly going in and out.

All I could hear: the internet was suspended. *Oh my God, how will I contact someone?*

I heard this commotion, people were running in and out of their homes, putting whatever they could in their vehicles. Children were asking, "What is this?"

Their moms and dads would only say, "We must move fast."

Wow! They are acting like they are afraid of something or someone. Something strange is taking place.

I just stood there in unbelief, wondering, *What should I do? I'll just go in the house, get dressed, and ride over to my sister's.* When I arrived, Patrice was in a panic.

"Can you hear that? Turn it up, Patrice, turn it up."

"Shh! Ok! I'm nervous too, that's why I came immediately."

"What's wrong with everyone?"

"You haven't heard? it's all over the television..."

"Oh, I didn't know, 'cause mine barely worked properly."

"They're coming for us" "Who, Peaches?"

"The doggone military."

"Why would they be coming for us?"

"Remember all we would hear about how things in the world would go south and there would be nothing any of us could do?"

"Yeah!"

"It's here, without a doubt. The money is no longer any good, so the government is saying the only way to control the people is to contain them. The preparation has been going on for years, evidently, for the most part. Quite a number of people thought this could never happen. Here we are, fighting for what's left of our lives.

"The government knows things are going to get very ugly, so they have prepared for this moment. It will be awful all over the globe, but there is nothing we can do except get out as quickly as we can. The only thing to do now is leave America before it's locked down, but we need passports to leave.

"Well, I prepared the best I could. I somewhat prepared for this moment, hoping this was just a joke. I always heard on the internet the money would be gone, martial law would be implemented... I saved, purchased some silver and gold. I was hoping we could use that until we get to where we are going."

"By the way, where are we going?"

"First, we have to get Mom and our brother..."

"What about Mame?"

"Oh, she and her family already left yesterday."

"Why are we just finding out now?"

"Well, you know where Mame worked... She handled big money, so she has always been ready in advance. I'm just glad that she and her family have gone. Who would have ever thought this would be happening in America? All I know is this type of thing was spoken about in the Bible. I guess people didn't believe and thought this would never come to be."

"I know, right? Time is up; it will be persecution on a large scale."

"Those FEMA camps that were talked about constantly on the internet… It looks like they're about to come true. I kind of thought this would happen, because the Bible doesn't lie at all. I'm sure people thought they would have more time to spiritually and emotionally prepare."

Patrice looked so scared and began to weep.

Peaches said, "I'm praying we can sustain all of this. We sure can't turn back the hands of time now, at this point… Who can at this point? Who can?"

While we were driving down the road, in my mind, I was thinking, *The day has come sooner than I would have ever known it would.* "I'm counting my blessings right now."

At least my sister was smart enough to think about the family. "My goodness, Patrice, to think of all the families that will be led to the FEMA camps!"

"Come on, Peaches, what are you doing?"

"Oh! I was thinking about all the people that will be trapped out here…"

"There is nothing we can do. Get a grip, please. We have no time to fall apart."

Patrice quickly asked, "What about your husband and children?"

"I meant to tell you, Pierre drove them down to Atlanta a couple of weeks ago. From there, Morocco… They may have a better chance, with all this chaos going on. We should be at the airport soon, as long as this traffic doesn't get more intense. I have been reading

Morocco is a place where a lot of people of color have migrated to. They must feel that would be a perfect place to survive. Patrice, how long do you think it will be before we arrive at the airport?"

"I don't know, Peaches. Soon, I pray. It seems others had the same idea; I suppose that's why the highways are so jammed."

Peaches and I were just so relieved to be getting out of America, even though this would be taking place globally. We were in the Most High hands at that point. No time to waste; this was definitely decision day for everyone. No one wanted to realize this was an epic moment in all of our lives. Life wouldn't be the same. Our fate would be decided on the choice we all would make... It couldn't be the wrong choice; it would determine where we spend eternity.

"Buckle up, we're in the ride of a lifetime. Do you think some will give in or give up? Because of the unknown, some may feel it would be better for them if they did."

"Yeah. For many, that could seem like the only answer."

I believe Peaches wasn't contemplating that thought. No, she wouldn't put her salvation on the line; the trust and faith she had in the Most High had forever been strong. Even to the very end, her endurance would be the fact to keep her going, no matter what.

"Let's see if we can get something on the radio."

"Do you hear that? Turn it up!"

"Oh my God, they're saying people everywhere are scattering to see what they can salvage to take out of their houses."

"Oh my! They say people everywhere are throwing things out of their houses, and they are burning and looting stores. What a time to be alive! It's like watching a movie on TV... This is all so real."

At this time of the day, the sky looked ominous. We were almost there. *What is this?*

Soldiers were crawling all over. *Is there no end to this madness? Why would they be here?*

Finally, we arrived at the airport. I couldn't believe what we witnessed out there.

You would think the soldiers were looking for terrorists. You never know! It hadn't been that long since Brazil went through something very horrific. We hadn't been checked for anything as of yet, probably just standard procedures.

"Caution is the word for the day, 'cause I am not trying to get my behind blown off. That wouldn't take much."

"Ha! ha! We need some laughter right about now. I'm so nervous!"

"I realize that. Just pray, Peaches."

"I've been doing that; haven't you noticed?"

Well, we made it inside. "Let's see what awaits us."

"There you go sounding all spooky, girl, please! This looks spooky. Take a good look at these people—they look spooked. They're holding their children for dear life."

"Get in line… Someone, help! Patrice, where is all that screaming coming from?"

"Up there in the front line."

"Wait a minute, in the same line we are in?"

"Yes!"

"This only means one thing: they only allow a certain amount of people to get in line so that they could grab a bunch at a time. You and I are going to make it out of this line without being noticed. Come on, Peaches, move fast."

We began to look for an exit, but nothing was nearby... We almost tripped over one another.

"I think I see a door over there. Let's go! I don't care if you run, run now! I didn't run track for nothing."

Peaches began reciting the Lord's Prayer right away. I told her there was nowhere out of there without us being seen by those soldiers. There happened to be two dumpsters. "We will get in those."

"Girl, are you crazy?"

"Crazy if we don't. I'll just be three feet away from you."

"I'm not going to get in there."

"You talked about getting your behind blown off... You just might this time! Now get in."

I saw some soldiers. "Ok! You don't have to tell me twice. If someone throws some scrap on us, I won't even care."

"I better peep out and make sure no one sees me getting out."

"Peaches! Peaches! Are you ok?"

"Yeah! it's about time. I started thinking we would be in there forever. Man, did it smell..."

Patrice went on to say, "Do you have any bright ideas?"

"Now you want to ask—"

"So what do you think?"

"I'm not sure. Um, let me see... We don't have a lot of choices at this point."

"We're walking!"

"Sounds good to me. I could have said the very obvious myself."

We started walking, and it was so hot, we could hardly breathe.

"We need some water... Where do you suppose we get that?"

"I don't know, anywhere but here... Come on, let's creep around real quiet until it's clear, then we can run as fast as we can. Getting on a plane is out of the question. We would just end up in one of those detention camps. I'm sure the people we saw are more than likely on their way as we speak."

"You ain't never lied, girl. They probably are."

We walked so far that from a distance, it looked like a cornfield. *Wow! It's eerie out here. I wonder where we are.*

I wanted to say I was afraid, but I didn't—that would have just gotten Patrice started again. There was a light about twenty feet ahead of us.

"I'm sure it's got to be getting late, Peaches."

It was difficult to see where the light was coming from, but it appeared to be some sort of house.

"Whatever! We can't stay out here all night. Eventually, someone is bound to see us. I hope whoever is behind those doors will be gracious enough to have a heart."

"I suppose you are right. The Lord has steered us in the right direction this far."

The darkness continued to cover the sky; it would be midnight soon. It was so strange, the feeling of being the only ones out in the wilderness. We got through the cornfields and approached the house. It reminded me of when we were little watching *The Wizard of Oz,* when Dorothy almost arrived to Emerald City.

Peaches knock on the door. "Ok! I'm kind of scared."

"I know!"

We both knocked. The voice from behind the door asked us, "Who's there?"

His Everlasting Word / 49

"It's my sister and I. We've been walking around all night, praying someone would help us. We're hungry and thirsty. Can you help?"

The man said, "Just a moment." He opened the door. He had the friendliest face. "What can I do for you ladies?"

"My name is Patrice, and this is my sister, Peaches."

"I see! Come on in. Follow me."

The kitchen was very large. "Have a seat, please."

We ate like it was our last meal on earth. He began to say, "My name is Paul. I live here alone… My wife passed a few years back, so it's just me out here. I'm sure you girls are tired. Let me show you to the room upstairs."

Paul looked like a nice man. Fear never entered our soul, and we were happy to be somewhere other than outside.

Morning came so abruptly. I could smell sausage cooking—it smelled delicious. I woke up Patrice, and we both headed downstairs.

"Hey, good morning! Did you girls sleep ok?"

"Yeah! We do thank you, Paul."

Paul had a smile on his face, as though we had known him a long time. "Could I offer you some breakfast?"

"Yes! Thank you, please."

Paul looked as though he wasn't very old. "So tell me, where are you girls trying to get to?"

"Morocco."

"Morocco… I see. There is probably a slight chance of that happening. We have to figure out how to make that happen. I was told there is military not far from here."

"We don't want to get caught and put in those detention camps." Peaches had her head down, talking to herself.

"Peaches, what are you saying?" I said.

"Oh, nothing... I was thinking out loud. I never thought in my wildest imagination that we would be going through something like this. This is the type of thing that my husband and I would hear about all over the internet. Here we are, living exactly what was said. My sister, Patrice, just found out today when I came over to her house."

Paul said, "I understand it all quite well now." He started getting all teary eyed. "I wish I could have joined Betsy when she passed. I'm absolutely all alone out here. I have no one except for some people I know down yonder. I would very much enjoy your stay until we can come up with a plan. Getting you to Morocco isn't going to be easy."

"Well, we know trying to leave will be difficult, but it's the only way to go 'cause if we stay, our lives are at stake."

Paul had a look on his face; he knew perfectly well what we could also be facing.

"You're right. Paul, are you thinking about going with us?"

"You girls will need a man around. You must realize this is going to take some careful planning. It'll take some detail."

"It ain't easy," Patrice said. "What about all of your belongings and memories?"

He just glanced at us ever so slightly, put his head down, and said, "My things don't matter now. If we don't hurry and come up with a plan, we might be in serious trouble."

There was a sigh of relief. We understood we had been blessed with someone that had a heart.

"We all need rest now! It has been a very long day."

His Everlasting Word / 51

"I agree! That sounds great to me. Maybe a master plan will come out better with some much-needed sleep."

By now, all I could hear were the crickets in the fields and the owl perched high in the tree on the side of the house. I listened to it for quite some time. Drifting off to sleep, I felt so peaceful. My eyes could no longer stay open. I wished this was all just a dream, but it wasn't.

When I awakened, it was already morning. The sun shined through the window so bright, with the shades of a rainbow in the cracks of the glass. Things you see that seem small, when knowing what's transpiring, leave an overwhelming pressure in your heart.

With all the beautiful things in this world turned cold, you wonder how it lasted this long. I guessed I couldn't answer that question myself. Times we were living in were changing in an astronomical rate; there was no turning back at this point; the Most High had spoken.

Many had read that times would change, and people would change for the worse one day... *We're here.*

It becomes unbearable when you try to put it all into perspective. *Could it be?* That's why the verse, in the Word says "Blessed are those that die now, they are more blessed that have gone on, that died in the Lord." It makes a great deal of sense. That's prophecy for you...

Here we are, caught right smack dab in all of it. Oh, wow! I had better get downstairs before Paul and Patrice come up with all the brainstormin' ideas.

"Good morning, everyone. How did the two of you sleep?"

Paul replied, "Not that well. I tossed and turned practically all night. As you both said, memories are something else... Hard not to think about them. I'll always have those."

Patrice began to look a little sad for Paul. "Hey, so what have you've put together?"

"Here are some escape routes moving out of the city; hopefully this will work."

I supposed it would nearly be impossible for Paul to know… Paul was what you call an old timer. Peaches was so excited, as though we were going on some adventure—well, actually, she was right, but fighting for our lives seem more appropriate to say. All and all, she wasn't far from the truth.

"Ok! Ladies, get your things together. We have to be on the way."

"That's fine, we're ready," we both said at the same time.

"Peaches, did you forget anything?"

"No! Did you?"

"Come on, girls, we have a very long journey ahead of us. The earlier, the better."

Peaches began to look doubtful. "Are you sure, Paul? Is daybreak the best time to leave? Won't we be more noticeable?"

"Mind you, we might, but didn't you say you want to get to Morocco?"

"Why, yes!" Peaches said. "That's where our family is."

Paul's eyebrows lifted high, like he was very curious about something. I didn't ask any more questions after that. I looked outside; Paul had already loaded up the supplies.

Patrice said, "Wow! Someone would have thought you were waiting on us to show up."

"Well, you never can be prepared enough these days."

"Yeah! I guess you're right."

Peaches had a very worried look on her face. I wondered what she was thinking. What he said made me a little uneasy. *No need to be concerned now; we are in it for the long haul.*

I have seen places in Minnesota, but this here was so lovely, I could have stayed for a long time.

"That must be Victor over on the side of the house, chopping wood."

There were two collies running in the yard, not a care in the world.

"Hey, Paul!"

"Hey!"

"How have you been?"

"Oh, I've been better!"

"I can't complain. Life could be worse, you know."

"Tell me about it."

"Are these the girls you texted me about?"

Peaches started nudging me in my side. Did she expect something?

"Paul, how did Victor know we were coming?"

"Oh, that! I texted him a while ago. I was glad that my cell phone worked; when we got to this part of the country, I wasn't sure. Let's get into the house. I suppose you girls are hungry by now."

He must have read our minds. I could have eaten one of those chickens hanging over by the fence. Maybe the chicken knew he was about to be dinner. Now, that wasn't far from the truth.

All we wanted to do was stretch out but first get some food.

"After supper, I'll show you ladies to your room. I hope it will be comfortable for you; that trip must have been hard on your backs.

The way he put that seemed strange, as though we had time to socialize. Maybe I was reacting because I was tried. There was no sign of other people living around. People in these rural areas always lived further away, compared to a larger, more populated city.

"Patrice, don't you find this whole scene a bit uncomfortable?"

"Yes! As a matter of fact, I do, because Paul's friend would have asked us where we are going. We will soon see! Maybe by the morning."

Peaches and I fell asleep so fast. We were still in one piece. There was talking coming from the drawing room, and it didn't sound like just the two of them.

"There's the ladies I was telling you about."

Immediately, the man and woman turned and focused hard on us.

"Listen, girls, this man and his wife, well, we were discussing what the safest route leaving Milwaukee would be."

Something was going on, and nervous was no longer the feeling we felt. At the same time, Peaches and I said, "What's going on? Why does it take so many people to help us get out of here?"

Paul knew we were very uneasy. The man almost made me laugh because he realized we were not happy about what we were being told, so he said, "There is no need to be concerned. My wife and I will take good care of the two of you."

I guess the sleep last night wasn't that great. We were still tired, and I didn't know what was going to happen. I couldn't help myself; I had to ask Paul why the lady and man were there.

He replied, "Just to give us some pointers on where the best route of traveling would be. Girls, when we get to Chicago, I'm going to do everything I can to get us on a plane, as you realize, we can't drive to Morocco. There must be some people at the airport I know from when I went overseas, so they will assist us."

"Man, Paul, you have all of this planned out. I was up half the night trying to come up with solutions."

"I told you girls I would be there for you, no matter what it took. Like I said, if I don't make it, I would make sure you'll be fine."

Peaches and I looked at one another. Paul was never going to go with us. I suppose when he left the airport, his days would come to an end.

"Here we are, girls, safe and sound." We turned around, and Paul looked very nervous and scared. One reality I'm sure of: Christ sent Paul into our lives.

The Most High blessed my sister and me with a casual friend, yet it was more than that—Paul was a man who had a heart of gold. Who could have asked for a better friend, even if it was just for a short time?

Just think, we had thought the opposite of him. I prayed he would be safe. We turned at the same time, but we could no longer see Paul fade off into the crowd.

It felt lonely even though Patrice and I had each other.

"What will we face when we touch down in Morocco?"

"You know something, Patrice, just until now, I never thought about it before."

"Do you think it might be possible that Paul could have been our guardian angel?"

"I have to say, the thought did cross my mind. It makes all the more sense right now. We hadn't run into trouble along the way, not once. There were soldiers all over the different cities we passed through. We managed to make it safely to the airport. We didn't have a chance to say goodbye to Paul. I believe he wouldn't have had it any other way."

That's one thing we will never know! Paul could have been our guardian angel Christ sent to us to get us safely out of America. The way he vanished into the crowd, it was as though he wasn't ever there. One thing is true: you'll never know if there is a blessing around the corner; that's the kind of faith Christ wants us to possess. You never know when you could be in the presence of an angel. No matter what adversity we may face in life, we must always be aware of the outcome, because when you put all your trust and faith in the Most High, He will always be there—even in that one dark day!

Resurrection

I long to see the dawning of the day
when I will hear Your calling as my spirit flies away,
for Christ controls all things in His infinite power.
The hour is sure to come!
You say you have time, but keep in mind,
you may not have time.
There is no time with the Father... Time is such a mystery.
We don't know when it comes and goes...
It's what you were told long ago.
The resurrection will be great.
Will we be the ones to stand at heaven's gate?
Those are the things we don't know for sure.
We must lift up our arms and bow our heads...
Give all praise to the King of heaven,
for He is waiting for His command from His Father,
who will sound the trumpet to keep you out of harm's way.
Give your life to Christ today...
There is no more time for delay.
So gather your hearts full of love and promise,
not knowing when the resurrection will occur.
Will you be ready for His arrival?
Keep holding fast and believe!
I am Christ, the only One who can set you free...
I am coming soon; My reward is with Me!
The resurrection is not just a dream for those who truly believe.

Do not go through not really knowing where your soul may go…
Let the Holy Spirit have His perfect will and way.
Serve the Most High today!

Silent Tears

Do you see? My love will go on for you, for all eternity.
Sometimes it feels like an impossible thing that only some share.
I'll keep mind, only you understand one thing that is true:
I'm loving you through and through.
I have given my heart to only you.
My soul cries silent tears! Can you hear?
No one knows our deep-seated feelings...
Constantly drowning in my silent tears,
tell me, what should I feel?
There is someone who knows me, made me to be
complete in Him.
I will only walk and talk to Him.
. My tears will fade away, like they have never been.
All cries, the Most High, realize, for He is wise...
The tears, I no longer have;
the fears, I no longer have...
When we hear, "Come,"
our silent tears are no longer here!

SISTAS

Sista, why are you cryin' a puddle of tears?
What's in this life that you fear?
The love you gave and lost...
Who's the boss of you?
You feel you can't go it alone...
What did you leave behind, a broken home?
Fragments of pieces of a dream?
Believe!
Sista, a diamond don't sparkle in the dark;
it's all about what's in your heart.
Love don't fade; it's all about,
what you put out, for all it's worth.
Give and take...
Is it your plan to stand at the pearly gate?
Your life isn't a mistake.
Sista, meditate on and live the life you have received.
Count your blessings along the way.
Wake up and live for today.
One thing that is true:
you have been given this one life to live.
Give your heart totally to our King.
There is a more meaningful life that only Christ can bring...
In this world where we live today,
It's not easy... I'd be the first to say.
To give your all and all,

will you be drawn to His call?
Select few only He knew...
Sista, stop cryin' a puddle of tears.
Stand up and be the woman He called.
Tomorrow is not promised for anyone.
Christ has the crown that will be placed.
Continue to live and run this race.

So Long Ago

So long ago, a man took a stand,
not to let anyone destroy His plan,
as time wrapped itself in its fullness, always with endurance.
So long ago, a man took a stand;
understand the love of this man.
As He's guiding our footsteps to master His plan,
never willing for any to die,
I see His teardrops as they fall from the sky.
So long ago, a man took a stand.
As the four winds blow, who's in control?
When the heavens roll up in a scroll
to read the names found in golden ink,
will your name be there? What do you think?
So long ago, a man took a stand,
taking a journey from a faraway place…
Oh, what a thought… Can you erase?
When you see His face all over the land, from place to place,
My Father in heaven sits up high
and looks down low; you can believe
He'll have the final blow.

Standing by the Ocean Side

Standing by the ocean side, watching Your creation around me,
seeing Your beauty that no one on this earth knew.
This could've only been You.
I'm alone and looking up,
wishing You would give me someone to love.
Just like You made space and the heavens above,
so complete, awesome, total power!

Submissive to Your will because I realize
there is no one that could hold this heart of mine…
You are my sunshine.
I'm standing by the ocean side.
I hear a voice, that says,
"Stand to the east and look!
This is My love I'm giving to you."
A wise man that stands,
the wisdom of time… He gives and lives
for the Most High… His guiding light!
Standing by the ocean side,
He is so intertwined with me.
This bottle of wine that's so divine…
Come walk with me!
We will live for the rest of our lives
walking in white and blue.
This is what Yah knew…

Full of love… No one will ever take it away!
Yah has given to you and me this day
a dream that became a reality,
Standing by the ocean side.

The Evidence of Love

Every time I wake up, the evidence of love is there.
Love is always in the air...
I have every right to care.
It's been given to me from my Creator,
so if it feels deep, I will stay on my knees,
day by day...
Praying for you and I.
The evidence of love is all around.
Don't be afraid to dream and realize
there is a better reality on the other side of life.
The evidence of love, we will soon see, surely!
You will believe when all of creation explodes
and comes together like never before!
Finally, reaching the Highest Love...
Yes! We will overcome; the Victory is won.
Join with me to feel the fire arising
within your souls... If you don't believe,
you'll never know the evidence of love.

The Light of Love

The light of love came and touched your heart,
letting you see
the creation of love that's meant to be.
In this life, you are born...
I'll love you forevermore.
This is the light of My love.
I will carry you, and you will know I am there.
You will figure out you haven't stood alone.
I have always been there.
You were told to open up your eyes
and see the inner mysteries hidden in Me.
I will only gather a chosen few...
What you call time, I am! Eternal.
There is none else like Me.
I am all that will ever be.
Pick up your cross and walk with me.
My spirit will not always strive with man.
Everyone is talking about this and that,
as of a matter of fact... Time is at hand!
There are many that don't know who I am!
Make ready your hearts; keep the faith.
Realize I'm coming soon... I will do a quick work!
Will you be in that number?
Or cast out into outer
darkness? I am the light of all eternity!
Keep faith in all you do! I will come for you...
I am the light of love.

The Longer You Hold My Heart

The longer you hold my heart, it only gets better with time.
We shared our ups and downs...
With love for you I've found
a love so deep, so right for me...
Please stay!
The longer you hold my heart, it only gets better with time.
In the still of the night, making love so nice.

My chocolate delight...
Waking up, seeing you beside me
has been so nice... Love so sweet!
This you can believe,
the longer you hold my heart.

TO ALL OF MY BROTHERS AND SISTERS

May you find our Savior Christ to be the One you need always in the years to come,
to enlighten you and be the beginning of truth to sustain you, keep you forever in His hands.
With your eyes continuously on the endurance of hope...
As we prepare to go into our kingdom for you and I, watch and pray, always.
Without ceasing, the Most High will lift you up!
Sorrow will get you down; at times, you may be cast down, but not destroyed.
There is forever hope in His everlasting arms!
For without Him, there is no hope. Without Him, you can do nothing.
Stay steadfast, with all you know to be truth.
Christ will gather you unto Himself... Love is the answer for all of us.
May Christ be the keeper of your soul. Shalom.

Turn Around, Turn Around

I'm reaching out My hands to you...
My love overflows any river and stream...
Wake up! Wake up! This is not a dream.
Turn around, turn around...
I, Yah, am here.
This life you should never fear...
The dawning of the day is drawing near.
Live and love everlasting... I, Yah, have forever known...
I will call My chosen home...
The last trumpet will sound...
Will love and faith be found?
Turn around, turn around...

Rejoice! Rejoice!
The time has come for all those sold out for me.
This will be the final call to be given
to those that held out to the end.
The crown of life—I, Yah, you will receive
because you believed...
You have won this race
because I am the Son, who laid out creation;
the sun, moon, and stars will soon be no more.
I will be the light of the of the entire world.
Come, enter the kingdom that will come;
Live forever as one.
Turn around! Turn around!
Keep calling out My name, and turn around.

Understanding

Life may be very hard for you...
Life may not mean anything to you.
Then if life is hard, there is someone in our lives;
He has always been there.
I'm speaking about Christ, the Creator of all things.
Some people aren't persistent enough—they give up!
Don't you want to feel the total fulfillment?
Take the time to think about this one thing;
you might feel better.
Our Heavenly Father knew what kind of life we would have.
This life you will understand;
you would be walking in the steps of Christ...
Striving to be the best someone you can be.
When you want to continue,
you feel lost out on hope.
Slowly come down too your knees and say,
"Father, I need Your help. I need you to lead me."
I promise, if you are sincere, He will show you the way.
If you don't believe in anyone but yourself, You may think,
I want what I want. This is my life.
I can choose to live in this world any way I want.
Not true! You would have been finished long ago.
We should all learn how to wait on the Lord.
Love is the answer...
It will forever be the most powerful thing in this universe.

Time waits for no one.
It looks like time is up!
When will you stand up
and be that woman or man that Christ gave us?
Time to decide… I choose the low road;
you may see someone that I can pick up along the way.
To choose the high road, I just might be too high-minded.
I'll just step over them; I feel I might get my clothes dirty.
If you are one of those who feel that way,
you would have put yourself in harm's way.
It would be a shame not to take the time to help your Brother
or Sister.
On the day when Christ returns, do you think He will know you?
If that is your way of wanting to live your life,
if you felt you had it all, if you didn't care,
then expect to live in the kingdom.
The Most High set the example.
He definitely died to be the example for all of us.
So I'll ask you, where will you spend eternity?
Heaven or hell? It's your choice.

WAITING

I've wondered so many times what love would be.
I said to myself I had to wait on thee,
to find out the love of the Lord that made me free.
I had to be ever loving…
My spirit was always longing for love;
I knew this within the deep recess of my womanly soul.
I had to give the Lord full control,
not take it in my tender hands.
With the love of the Lord,
I will find that man…
Someone who is truthful and understands
I want to be your friend,
just like a ring is round and has no end…
That's where our destiny begins.
I want to be your friend,
where we can sit and watch
the tides roll in,
feeling the rays of the setting sun dancing across our face
as we sit here enjoying God's beauty and grace
I want to be your friend…
The kind that lasts and never ends.

Where Are You, My Brother?

Where are you, my brother?
And yo' queen soul gifted mother?
Should we hide in the twilight hour?
We still have the power?
Come up and ask me what I think;
our insight is unique.
Sitting on the milky way
while you believin' yo' dreams are thown away...
Where are you, my brother?
And yo' queen soul gifted mother?
The heavens are high; I don't have too fantasize
or ask any reasons why.
Does this mean they will flow away?
Black brothers and sisters, we're here to stay.

Where Did Our Love Go?

Some things are better left unsaid
when you have been down the road of disappointment.
In the beginning, it was easy to believe...
Love and life seemed to be meant for me and you.
Life went by us so quickly...
Forgetting how to live and dying within.
Where did our love go?
We got comfortable, never to realize we needed one another.
Where did our love go?
Our hearts no longer beating as one...
I have been here unnoticed, undone.
You still want to say our love is as one...
I want to say, "Set my heart free."
I see you don't believe...
I will stop cryin' the tears you won't see!
You will continue to say...
"Where did our love go?"

With Open Arms

I climb to the highest mountain top...
and see a vision of beauty only You bring.
Then something happens within me:
a voice so profound and clear.
I hear You say, "Come and stay with Me forever.
You are for this day.
All of your tears I wipe away.
You are no longer part of this life...
With open arms, I will give to you that crown of life
for all those who hear the sound of My voice...
Come up hither and receive all that's in My heart.
With open arms, I have set your soul far apart!
You have searched for Me deep in your heart,
while were young.
Nothing in this life can be won.
With open arms, I will carry you through the dreadful storm...
With open arms."

Without You

Hold close the memories we shared…
Don't throw them all away.
Without you, I'm like a ship tossed and turned about
You're the anchor of my heart, sturdy and strong.
Without you, how can I go wrong?
There's a mystery of our love
only given once…
Without you, I can give my heart so free
to you, sharing love captured in space and time…
Without you, I'll never find you by my side.
Nothing would matter, inside I realize
without your arms, without you, how can I breathe?
Without you near, there's no reason to dream.
It's only you I need, this you can believe…
Without you…

Worthy of Love

Am I worthy of Your love?
The days seem to close around me;
Sometimes I can hardly breathe!
Christ understands what's inside me.
I was destined to be Yours; You are mine...
Worthy of love.
If I didn't have You beside me to guide me,
I'd be lost. We hurt way deep within,
like a well that has no end.
I'm worthy of love! We smile with a slight disguise...
All along, I'm falling and falling
to the end of a mountain.
Climb... I wanna know!
Am I worthy of Your love?
We ask daily when we get on our knees and pray.
Please don't take Your love away...
Here comes the rain,
so divine and sure.
The pureness of Your love... My Savior!
Is that You I see, breaking through
where there was never time and space?
With joy unspeakable, You call my name.
Everything fades away...
All I see is You! Carry me to a place...
I now understand! Tears of golden raindrops!

I know it must be You...
Christ, our Savior, it's always been You.
We then comprehend, in the end!
Our faith, trust, and love
make us complete in the Most High's love.
No longer will we ask,
"Am I worthy of Your love?"
After all, it has all been said and done.
I am worthy of Your love!
You, Christ, our Savior.

Quotes for the Day

When You entered my life, the stages of something new no one could have shown me... With time spent, You will always be that someone new, when I spend my time honoring and trusting only You. Christ, You are all that I hope for.
Don't wait on a miracle if you don't believe in the One who created them.
It's easier to give up than to stop believing.
Why trust anyone when you don't believe in anything?
Don't laugh when you forgot to cry.
Pray for today... Hope for tomorrow.
When I give you wings to fly, will you believe I have always existed?
No one can tell you Christ doesn't exist when all you have to do is look in the mirror.
The softness of your touch will remind me that I am loved.
Your kisses speak colors—a rainbow with no end.
Life is like walking through the clouds when I know Christ will catch me when I fall.
It's easier to remember a memory than to remember a dream.
Why should I give up when all I have to do is trust in You?
If there was no love, there would be no You.
If you hold God's hand, that is your reason to believe.
Trust is earned a thousand different ways... It's better to trust what you can't see than to believe in what you can't.

Christ rides the storm clouds to remove all evil in the path of your way.
The storm clouds cease at His call when He removes the evil in your way.
I'm so over the moon in love with You. As long as I have You, the light of love will never leave my heart. As long as I have you, words are all I have, until You hold me in Your arms.
Let the sun shine within your soul.
I've dreamed of you in my past life. Maybe you are my future.

The gift of love that You have given is only part of Your mystery.
If you hear a soft voice, it doesn't mean it's your imagination…
It's your Father trying to get your attention.
Remembering a dream becomes your reality….
Surprise someone you don't know by saying, "Life is good… There will always be someone to love."
I pray for you more than anything I know in this life, that you will see God for yourself… I don't know you, but God does, for He is love.

Epilogue: Let's Be Real

There are different sects of religion in the world, and I believe there is something to say about every religion. I myself have traveled down that road and thought I was following the truth, until six years ago. Looking back on that road of decision in my life, I won't say I have any regrets. I have learned to totally trust in our heavenly Creator because I realize there is something spiritual happening in the earth—no one that can see can deny that fact.

The Most High knows what's best for each and every one of us. There is no sense in arguing whose religion is correct or righteous because, at the end of the day, did you live your life for Ahaya and His Son, Jesus Christ, and did you follow the Ten Commandments of the Most High God? I will faithfully admit, His name is Ahaya, and His Son's name is Yashaya. I know many would not trust or believe in those names, as I've stated, but I will not argue the point. We are not supposed to do that.

When it comes down to it, everyone has their belief and opinion. For many, will you continue honor the Sabbath Day, which is Saturday, as well as the Ten Commandments, given by the Most High? Ask yourselves, why would He give commandments? It became justified to give them, just like the law of the land was given by the law givers, which is truly the same. We all have a high calling in our lives, and we are not to live in any kind of way. As a people, we feel we have the right to live any kind of way.

When there is one, true God, who made us and gave us all life, He alone has the power and is able to take away life. The power is in His hands to let that be. So do you really feel we have the right to live our lives in any kind of way that we see fit? No! Not at all. A very few compared to the many people in the universe have never felt that it was any truth to serve anyone other than themselves. There is no reason to believe in a magnitude of such different nationalities that have lived on this earth throughout space and time.

So many people don't understand this is the very fabric of truth. At least, look into it and see—that is, if you want—and know we must all believe in the Ten Commandments. There is a hell, because if there wasn't, Hollywood wouldn't make so many movies about it. Hell is a real place; it didn't just come from a thought. Would you say your life is better with or without His commandments? Would you say, "I don't believe in them, let alone this Creator of heaven and earth people speak of." Well, if so, look at the state of this world today. It's definitely not a life-sustaining world with change of the betterment for humanity.

The commandments are not some words that should be distasteful; they are words of wisdom, so worthy that we all should want to abide by them. Unfortunately, that isn't the case... Ask yourselves, will you sow the seed of unrighteousness, or reap the seed of disobedience? That is a choice we all have to make.

I must say, in my heart of hearts, I can only say what's on my heart, not being condescending in any way. I truly love you, whether I know you or not. That is the second greatest commandment of all—love thy neighbor as thyself. Honestly, it would be beautiful if everyone felt the same. Most people would agree that it's not easy. What a better world we could live in.

We all live in a state of emergency of a choice to make. Rest assured that when that day comes, it will not come as a surprise too many. To any preacher, minister, and Rabbi who ever feels it's their responsibility to tell the truth, I need not ask, "What's your point?" I'm not here to judge any man, woman, or child. I leave that to the only true God of heaven. That is His decision, not mine. Have you told your flock what's to come and prepared for the greatest event to take place real soon? When they are told the full truth, then they will have an idea of where they will spend eternity. There is a surety that is written in the Book of Life—and death—for each and every one of us. If you can't see, or if you don't want to, trust and have faith... He can move any mountain in your life. His coming will be known to all. Watch! Life events will be revealed right before your very eyes. Search the Scriptures for yourself. Make a stand, be true to you, examine what's going on around you, and look at the news. Truth, love, and faith will be the only thing standing at the end of the day.

May our Father be the true source and guide you forever. Until His blessed appearance.

www.ingramcontent.com/pod-product-compliance
Ingram Content Group UK Ltd.
Pitfield, Milton Keynes, MK11 3LW, UK
UKHW022222230426
12048UKWH00016BA/1002